1st Edition

ISBN 979-8-218-56614-2

Dedication

To those who have stumbled and found the strength to stand again, this book is for you. To my family, whose love has been my foundation, and to God, who has been my guide through every step and every setback. May we all keep moving forward in faith and resilience.

About the Author

Jacob Brown's journey from the intense NFL fields to international stages and boardrooms is a testament to resilience and reinvention. Today, as a dynamic entrepreneur, sought-after speaker, and first-time author, Jacob inspires audiences to meet challenges head on and redefine their relationship with failure. Beyond his achievements in sports, Jacob co-founded Varlo, a leading brand in cycling and triathlon apparel, bringing his background in sports and creativity to the world of endurance athletes.

A three-time TEDx speaker, Jacob was recognized as one of the "40 Under 40" in 2015, with insights featured in Forbes, Wall Street Journal, and Good Morning America. Top brands and institutions like Intel, Meta, LinkedIn, Dallas Cowboys, UPS, Stellantis, University of Notre Dame, University of Michigan, University of Wisconsin, and his alma mater, Central Michigan University, have been captivated by his talks on resilience, transformation, and purpose.

Jacob's mission is more than motivational speaking; he advocates for a transformative approach to life through his #FailForward philosophy. His widely shared posts and videos encourage others to see setbacks as opportunities and reframe challenges as growth experiences. From LinkedIn to live stages, his message has inspired thousands worldwide to turn failures into fuel for progress.

Born and raised in Saginaw, MI, Jacob is the middle child of seven and the first in his family to earn a full athletic scholarship, which took him to Central Michigan University. There, he played college football for five years, majored in graphic and web design, and explored his love of art. His career path eventually led him to serve as a creative director in corporate America for nearly 15 years before he became a full-time entrepreneur. Beyond his professional life, Jacob is a devoted family man, proud husband, and father of four. His favorite pastimes include grilling, baking, fishing, and the occasional video game session with his kids.

Jacob's story is a reminder that life's setbacks don't define us - how we respond to them does. Through his experiences, he's shown that anyone can fail forward, discovering purpose, strength, and resilience along the way.

Table of Contents

Introduction

Life is often painted as a smooth journey toward achieving our dreams. But the truth is, life is more like a wild rollercoaster full of ups and downs. My path, much like yours, has had its fair share of bumps. Before I made my way to the NFL, my dream playground, I heard something from my aunt that stuck with me: "Fail Forward."

I didn't really get what this phrase meant until life threw a bunch of tough times my way: battles with dark thoughts, getting caught up in addiction, going through a painful divorce, and even facing homelessness. Each hurdle was a hard reminder that our road to growth and success often includes failures and setbacks.

But here's the cool part: with every stumble, I learned something new; with every fall, I found a way to get back up stronger. This idea of failing forward became my guiding light through these rough times, showing me the way to better days. It's the mix of all these hard times and the never-give-up spirit that brought this book, *Fail Forward Mentality*, to life.

As you flip through this book, you'll discover a journey filled with personal stories, actionable insights, and strategies to help you embrace a fail forward mentality. Each chapter explores a key area of life, from relationships and career to health and finances, offering guidance on transforming setbacks into opportunities for growth. Alongside these lessons, you'll find a collection of my favorite 100 motivational quotes, each a spark of hope to keep you moving forward when life feels heavy. This book is a source of courage and resilience, reminding you that challenges are steppingstones, and with the right mindset, every stumble can bring you closer to the person you're meant to be.

Fail Forward Mentality is more than just a book - it's a journey. Every page you turn is a step closer to discovering your own resilience and strength. This book is a shoutout to the unbeatable spirit in each of us, a call to take on our challenges, learn from them, and keep moving forward.

Here's to a journey of resilience and growth as you dive into these pages, carrying a Fail Forward Mentality into every chapter of your life.

CHAPTER 1

Fail Forward Mentality

"Failure isn't the end; it's the foundation of every comeback."

Fail Forward Mentality

August 17, 2009 was a day that forever changed my life. I remember it like it was yesterday. It was a Monday. The weather forecast was sunny, with a high of 85° and a low of 74°. The song of the year that year was "I Got A Feeling" by the Black Eyed Peas. The most popular baby names for boys in 2009 were Ethan, Michael, and, of course, Jacob. For girls, Emma, Olivia, and Sophia. Famous celebrity birthdays that day were Robert De Niro, Donnie Walberg, and Sean Penn.

That morning, the moon was still showing in the sky. It was a waning crescent moon that day, meaning that the moon was in its last phase, only showing a sliver of its light.

The waning crescent wasn't just a random phase, it was a mirror of where I was that morning. Worn down, barely hanging on, with only a sliver of light left. But what I didn't realize then was that the waning crescent is also a sign of transformation. It's the reminder that darkness isn't forever...it's just the transition before a new beginning. The moon disappears for a moment, only to reappear as something new.

And maybe, just maybe, that was what I needed to do too.

I remember these details so vividly because this was the day I'd planned to end my life.

I remember leaving the house around 6 a.m. headed to work and hoping it was raining. It was supposed to rain. I actually prayed for rain.

I'd just turned 26 and at that point in my life, I felt like the biggest failure. I'd gotten married way too young and was in a failing marriage. I had two sons at the time and felt like a failing father. I'd failed out of college, seeking my dream to play in the NFL, which also failed. At this point, I had failed jobs, failed businesses, failed relationships, and, from what I felt deep inside, a failed life.

Growing up, the dream wasn't just mine, it was everyone's dream for me. Football wasn't just a game, it was my ticket to everything: respect, stability, success, and pride.

There was no plan B that seemed as real as Plan A, and every stumble along the way felt like a crack in the identity I'd built for myself. When I failed out of college, it meant more than just leaving school. It meant losing the vision of the man I thought I would be.

Every day felt like I was drowning just a little more. I went to bed hoping that maybe the next morning I'd wake up with the strength to keep going. But every sunrise felt heavier than the last. I tried to smile for my kids, fake it for my friends, and act strong for my employees, but the weight of feeling like I was disappointing everyone ate at me.

The hardest part? I couldn't figure out how to ask for help.

The pressure I felt was just too much, so I'd created a plan. That morning, while on my way to work, my plan was to swerve around a sharp corner by a lake, hit a large tree, and fall into the lake as though it were an accident. I didn't want anyone, especially my children, to believe I'd intentionally left them. That would have been selfish, right?

So, as I left the house, hoping it was raining, I made the decision to go through with it. As I was approaching the large tree by the lake, I sped up, and then something happened. About 30 yards from the tree, I heard a voice.

"Jacob, fail forward."

This was the voice of my aunt, Faith.

Failing forward was a concept I'd learned from her just three years prior to that monumental day. I was visiting her in Atlanta prior to the 2006 NFL Draft, when she asked me a simple question.

"Jacob, what happens if football doesn't work out?"

I was stunned at her question but answered, "Well, if football doesn't work out, I'll just fall back on my degree." She responded, "If you are ever going to fall or fail, always fall or fail forward."

That statement slapped me right in the face, because in all my years of playing the game of football, I was always taught that when you got tackled, you fell forward. When you fall forward in football, you gain extra yards, and if you get tackled on the one-yard line but fall forward – touchdown!

This is a concept that I have learned to apply to my daily life. From relationships to business ventures to careers to parenting to even new cooking recipes, I fail forward.

Whether I succeed or fail, I use the failure, adversity, and hard times we all inevitably go through to learn lessons, grow thicker skin, and ultimately help others.

Looking back on my life, I can see how every high, every low, every twist, and every turn brought me to where I am today. There were times when I couldn't make sense of what was happening, moments that felt like they would break me. But now, with the benefit of hindsight, I realize that truly, everything happens for a reason.

One scripture that has become a guiding light for me is Romans 8:28: "And we know that all things work together for good to those who love God, to those who are called according to His purpose." Those words have helped me hold on when life has felt uncertain. They've reminded me that even the struggles, disappointments, and delays have a purpose woven into a bigger plan. Sometimes, we have to go through seasons of hardship to grow, to learn, or to become the people we're meant to be. We're refined by the process, becoming stronger, wiser, and more compassionate along the way.

This scripture is more than just a comforting phrase; it's a promise that no experience is wasted. Every experience, every setback, and every tear is transformed into something that ultimately serves a greater purpose. And for me, this understanding has been the foundation of resilience. I know that even if I don't understand why in the moment, I can trust that it's all leading me somewhere good, somewhere I'm meant to be.

Hearing my aunt's voice in that moment was like a lifeline. I hadn't thought about her words in years, but somehow, in my darkest moment, they'd resurfaced. It's strange how the mind works like that...how a memory from years ago can find you exactly when you need it the most. At the time, I didn't fully understand what it meant to fail forward, but the voice was enough to make me pause. And in that pause, everything changed.

August 17, 2009 was the day that I realized failure didn't have to be the end. In fact, it can be the beginning. J.K. Rowling, a British author and philanthropist, says, "Rock bottom became the solid foundation on which I rebuilt my life."

That day was rock bottom for me, but I didn't know what life had in store and the failures I would endure for years to come.

To this day, I still fail, but I now use failure as fuel. This is what I call a fail forward mentality, and it is something I do daily.

Always fail forward.

CHAPTER 2

Why Fail Forward?

"Failure is the fuel for forward motion. Each setback is a lesson, each stumble a step toward strength and purpose."

Why Fail Forward?

Failure is inevitable. No matter how talented you are, how well you plan, or how hard you work, life will present challenges, setbacks, and disappointments. But the truth is, it's not the failure itself that determines the course of your life - it's how you respond to it.

This is where the fail forward mentality becomes essential.

The fail forward mentality is about embracing failure as part of the process, not as an endpoint. When you learn to reframe failure as a necessary step toward growth, it no longer feels like the end of the road. Instead, it becomes the momentum for your next step forward. Without it, you might find yourself paralyzed by fear, avoiding action altogether, waiting for the perfect conditions that will never come.

There's a story about a Chinese farmer who once lost his horse. When the neighbors heard, they came by to sympathize, saying, "Such bad luck!" But the farmer simply replied, "Maybe."

The next day, the lost horse returned with several wild horses. The neighbors, thrilled, exclaimed, "What good fortune!" Yet again, the farmer replied, "Maybe."

Not long after, the farmer's son attempted to ride one of the wild horses, only to be thrown off and break his leg. The neighbors came to offer their condolences for this misfortune, but the farmer once again said, "Maybe."

A few weeks later, the army came through the village to recruit young men. Because of his injury, the farmer's son was spared from conscription. The neighbors, amazed, said, "Such good luck!" And, as always, the farmer simply replied, "Maybe."

In China, when someone faces a setback, they often say, "Sai Weng Shi Ma," a reminder of "The Old Man Who Lost His Horse." It's a way of acknowledging that what seems like misfortune may hold a hidden blessing. This phrase encourages people to see beyond the immediate difficulty, understanding that it's often our perspective that gives events their true power over our spirit.

This story illustrates the unpredictability of life. What appears as failure can sometimes turn into an unexpected blessing. The Chinese farmer understood that life wasn't happening to him - it was happening for him.

The fail forward mentality encourages us to take every step knowing that what appears as a setback may simply be one part of a larger picture. The truth is, progress requires risk, and risk comes with the possibility of failure. If you avoid failure, you avoid progress.

One of the biggest dangers of the fear of failure is paralysis. Perfectionism tricks us into thinking we need everything to be just right before we can act. But waiting for the perfect moment only keeps you stuck. It's not perfection that leads to success, it's movement. The fail forward mentality gives you permission to take imperfect action, knowing that every step, even the missteps, moves you closer to your goal.

The beauty of failing forward lies in the resilience it builds. Every time you get back up after falling, you strengthen your ability to handle life's inevitable challenges. Resilience is a muscle, and failure is the workout that strengthens it. Without failure, success can be fragile. When things come too easily, we don't develop the emotional stamina needed to endure future setbacks. But when you've experienced failure and learned to rise from it, success becomes more sustainable. You know you can handle whatever comes your way because you've proven it to yourself time and time again.

Failure is also a powerful source of innovation. Some of the greatest breakthroughs in history came not from initial success but from repeated failure. The setbacks forced people to pivot, think creatively, and find new solutions they never would have discovered otherwise. When you allow failure to guide you, it becomes a tool for growth rather than an obstacle.

You stop asking "Why me?" and start asking "What's next?"

Another reason the fail forward mentality matters is because it frees you from the fear of judgment. Many people are so afraid of what others will think that they never take the risks that could lead to transformation. But when you internalize the idea that failure is part of the process, you stop worrying about appearances. You are not your failures...you are the person who keeps moving, keeps learning, and keeps growing, no matter what. This kind of freedom is rare, and it's essential for anyone striving to live a meaningful life.

Failure also deepens your empathy for others. When you've faced setbacks yourself, you become more understanding of other people's struggles. You realize that everyone is carrying something, and no one's path is as smooth as it might appear from the outside. This empathy strengthens your relationships and helps you connect with others in more meaningful ways.

Your story of failing forward can even become the spark that inspires someone else to keep going.

A fail forward mentality also teaches you who you really are. It strips away the superficial layers of success and makes you confront your core values and identity. In those moments when nothing is going right, you learn what truly matters to you and where your inner strength lies. Success may feel good, but it's in failure that you discover your grit, your resilience, and your purpose.

Success without failure is not only rare but also dangerous. When people succeed too easily, they can develop a false sense of security, thinking they'll always come out on top. But life doesn't work that way. True success is built on the foundation of lessons learned through trial and error. It's not about avoiding failure but learning how to use it to your advantage.

This mindset also makes you a lifelong learner. Instead of seeing setbacks as roadblocks, you start to view them as opportunities to grow. Every mistake becomes a lesson. Every obstacle becomes a challenge to overcome. With a fail forward mentality, you focus less on achieving perfection and more on becoming better than you were yesterday.

The fail forward mentality gives you a new definition of success. It's not just about reaching a goal but about becoming the kind of person who can handle whatever life throws your way. It's about embracing the journey, knowing that every misstep, wrong turn, or failed attempt is part of the process of becoming who you were meant to be.

In the end, adopting this mindset isn't just about achieving more; it's about living more freely, more courageously, and more authentically. When you stop fearing failure, you unlock the courage to take risks, try new things, and pursue dreams you never thought possible. You discover that failure is not the opposite of success - it's the path to it. And with every fall, you learn to rise stronger, smarter, and more determined than before.

This is why the fail forward mentality matters. It's not just a strategy for success...it's a way of life. It's about accepting that failure will happen, and when it does, you'll use it to propel yourself forward. No matter how hard you fall, you'll always have a reason to get back up. And when you live with that kind of mindset, there's no limit to what you can achieve.

CHAPTER 3

7 Ways to Grow a Fail Forward Mentality Daily

"Growth is the sum of small, courageous steps taken every day, with failure as the fuel that moves you forward."

7 Ways to Grow a Fail Forward Mentality Daily

Having a fail forward mentality isn't just a one-time decision...it's a daily practice. It requires intentional habits, thoughtful reflection, and conscious effort to reframe challenges as opportunities. Shifting your mindset to embrace failure as fuel for growth won't happen overnight, but with the right strategies, you can cultivate this approach and make it a part of your everyday life. This chapter offers practical steps and tools you can use to develop a fail forward mentality and sustain it, even when things get tough.

1. Start Your Day Shapes Your Mindset

The way you begin your morning influences how you handle the challenges that will inevitably arise. When you approach the day with intentionality, you're more likely to see obstacles as opportunities rather than setbacks. One way to do this is through affirmations or mantras - simple statements that prime your brain for resilience. Repeating phrases like, "Every challenge is a chance to grow" or "Mistakes mean I'm trying" helps shift your focus from perfection to progress.

Another powerful practice is visualizing potential obstacles. This skill was instilled in me by my mom, who taught me the art of visualization when I was young. Before every game, she would have me lay on my back, close my eyes, and envision myself scoring the game-winning touchdown, hitting a home run, or sprinting across the finish line. Through this simple yet profound exercise, she showed me the power of seeing success before it happened.

As adults, we can apply that same power by spending a few quiet minutes each morning, imagining how our day might unfold, including the moments that might not go according to plan. Picture yourself responding to those moments with grace and determination. This mental rehearsal makes it easier to navigate challenges when they arise. Finally, journaling with intention helps set the tone for your day. Write down one recent failure and what it taught you, along with small steps you can take today to keep moving forward, even if it means risking more mistakes. Starting your day with these practices builds a mental foundation to help you act with a growth mindset no matter what the day brings.

2. Reframe Setbacks as They Happen

Throughout the day, things will not always go according to plan. A fail forward mentality means learning to pause in these moments, take a breath, and reframe setbacks in real-time. This practice can be the difference between giving up and moving forward. One of the first steps is to catch negative self-talk. When something goes wrong, it's easy to think, "I knew I wasn't good enough" or "Why does this always happen to me?" Instead, try replacing these thoughts with constructive ones: "This is part of the process" or "What's the lesson here?"

Ask yourself powerful questions to reframe setbacks: **What is this experience trying to teach me? How can this make me stronger for the next step?**

Sometimes, it helps to name the opportunity out loud. When I was spiraling in doubt over my failed dreams, it was my aunt's voice reminding me to fail forward that shifted my perspective. Now, whenever I hit a roadblock, I practice naming the opportunity: "This delay is teaching me patience" or "This rejection is refining my next approach." Reframing setbacks on the spot keeps you grounded and allows you to maintain momentum, even when frustration creeps in.

3. Step Outside Your Comfort Zone Every Day

Building a fail forward mentality requires daily effort in stepping beyond what feels comfortable. Small risks may not always lead to success, but they build resilience and help you grow. One way to do this is by setting "stretch goals." These are goals that push you slightly beyond your current abilities...goals that might not guarantee success but promise growth.

Taking risks doesn't always have to be monumental. It can be as simple as trying a new recipe, making an uncomfortable phone call, or starting a conversation you've been avoiding. When I felt trapped by my failures, I realized the only way to move forward was to keep experimenting, even if it meant stumbling along the way. Keep a record of the risks you take each day, no matter how small. This builds momentum and helps you reflect on your progress, even when you encounter setbacks. Daily risks remind you that failure isn't something to fear, it's part of the path forward.

4. Celebrate Failure as Part of the Process

Celebrating failure may sound strange, but it's one of the most powerful ways to reinforce the fail forward mentality. When you shift your focus from outcomes to effort, you realize that growth matters more than winning. One way to do this is by creating a "failure log." This can be a journal or a digital document where you record your failures and the lessons learned. Over time, this log becomes a powerful reminder of how far you've come - not just through successes but through setbacks as well.

Sharing your stories of failure with others helps, too. Talking openly about mistakes normalizes failure and reduces the shame that often accompanies it. I've found that when I share my story - including the darkest moments like that day by the lake - others feel less alone in their own struggles. Lastly, find ways to reward effort, not just results. Sometimes the win lies in the fact that you tried, even if it didn't work out as planned. Acknowledge your courage in taking the risk - it's what makes failing forward possible.

5. Surround Yourself with People Who Inspire Growth

The people you surround yourself with have a profound impact on your mindset. To stay consistent with a fail forward mentality, it's essential to seek out individuals who encourage learning, risk-taking, and growth. These might be friends, mentors, or colleagues who will lift you up when things don't go as planned. At the same time, it's important to limit your exposure to those who discourage you or reinforce fear of failure.

Consider joining communities where people openly share stories of both success and failure. Being part of growth-minded groups reminds you that setbacks are a normal part of any journey. Just as I had my aunt Faith to encourage me, having people around you who believe in the power of failing forward amplifies your courage. Surround yourself with those who make you feel like it's okay to stumble, as long as you keep moving forward.

6. Practice Gratitude for Challenges and Setbacks

Gratitude isn't just for the easy moments. Developing a fail forward mentality means learning to be grateful for the hard ones too. At the end of each day, take time to reflect on one thing you're grateful for, even if it was a difficult experience. This practice rewires your brain to see value in every situation, good or bad.

It may feel strange at first, but try thanking your setbacks. For example: "Thank you, missed promotion, for teaching me patience" or "Thank you, failed relationship, for helping me discover what I value." Practicing gratitude for challenges shifts your focus from frustration to growth. The sooner you learn to see the gifts within failures, the easier it becomes to keep moving forward with purpose.

7. Reflect and Adjust Every Day

Developing a fail forward mentality is a lifelong process that requires regular reflection. At the end of each day, ask yourself key questions: What did I learn from today's challenges? Where did I show resilience? What can I do differently tomorrow? These small reflections will keep you aligned with your goals and mindset.

Use each day as an opportunity to make micro-adjustments. If something didn't go as planned, identify one small change you can implement tomorrow. Tracking your wins and lessons together ensures you see that both successes and failures are part of the same journey. Regular reflection helps you stay grounded, reminding you that every experience, whether it feels like a win or a loss, contributes to your growth.

CHAPTER 4

In Relationships

"Strong relationships aren't built on perfection but on vulnerability, trust, and the courage to grow together."

In Relationships

Relationships – they can be hard, right? They're one of life's biggest sources of joy, growth, and, sometimes, pain. We all want connections that lift us up and make life better, but even the best relationships bring their share of heartache. They push us to our limits, show us parts of ourselves we might not want to see, and challenge us to grow. And while setbacks in relationships can hurt, each one is a chance to fail forward, to learn, and to get closer to the kind of connections we really want.

Think of it this way: relationships are like mirrors. They reflect back what's good in us and what we still need to work on. Sometimes, we see qualities we're proud of. Other times, we face stuff we'd rather ignore. But here's the thing: when we start looking at each relationship as a lesson, we can find value in every ending, every fight, every awkward moment. Instead of asking, "Why did this happen to me?" we can start asking, "What can I learn here?" That's failing forward.

Failing forward in relationships doesn't mean dodging pain or pretending things are fine. It means accepting that every connection, whether it lasts a lifetime or just a season, has something to teach us.

Embracing Vulnerability

Let's be real: vulnerability is tough. Opening up to others means risking judgment, rejection, or misunderstanding. But vulnerability is the heart of real connection, and every time we're brave enough to show up as ourselves, we're taking a step forward. Sure, sometimes it doesn't end the way we hope

- a friendship might drift apart, or a relationship might fizzle out. But each time we're honest about who we are, we learn that our worth isn't defined by other people's reactions. It's about being true to ourselves.

Vulnerability is a big part of failing forward in relationships. The more we let ourselves be seen, the stronger we become. And hey, even if things don't work out, at least we know we showed up as our true selves.

Learning Through Letting Go

Letting go is hard. Sometimes, though, failing forward means knowing when a relationship has run its course. This isn't about blaming anyone; it's about being honest with ourselves. Maybe it's a friendship that's no longer supportive, or a romantic relationship that's drifted. Letting go doesn't mean we've failed. It means we're brave enough to admit when something isn't right for us anymore.

Learning to let go teaches us that we deserve relationships that feel good and bring out the best in us. It's about growth over comfort and honesty over obligation.

Setting Boundaries

Relationships are better with healthy boundaries. And yet, setting boundaries can feel awkward, especially if you're a people-pleaser. But boundaries are there to protect your peace, energy, and time. They let you show up fully for others because you're not stretched too thin.

Setting boundaries is failing forward because it's a way of valuing yourself and your needs. It's about letting others know what you need, so your relationships can be based on respect. And that's how you build connections that feel good, not draining.

Embracing Imperfection

No relationship is perfect. Mistakes happen, missteps happen, and misunderstandings are pretty much guaranteed. But failing forward in relationships means accepting these flaws. Our relationship partners don't need us to be perfect; they just need us to be willing to learn.

When we mess up, instead of beating ourselves up, we can use it as a learning moment. Relationships teach us how to give grace to ourselves and others. And that grace is what makes relationships worth it in the end.

Growing Together, Even When Apart

Sometimes, people come into our lives for a season and then move on. It's tough, especially if we wanted them to stay. But every person who crosses our path plays a part in our growth, whether they're in our lives forever or just for a little while.

When a relationship ends, it's easy to focus on what we lost. But what if we looked at it as, "What did I gain?" Every connection has something to teach us, even the ones that don't last. That's failing forward: moving ahead with gratitude instead of regret.

Choosing Growth Over Resentment

Not all relationships end peacefully. Sometimes words are said, and hurt lingers. But failing forward means choosing growth over resentment. Holding onto anger only keeps us stuck. Letting go of bitterness frees us to move on, staying open to new connections that feel good.

Forgiveness doesn't mean forgetting what happened. It means choosing to not let it weigh us down. It's about deciding that peace is worth more than staying stuck in the past.

Embracing a Fail-Forward Mindset in Love

Love can be amazing, and it can also be one of the biggest challenges we face. Every heartbreak, unreturned crush, or unmet expectation is a chance to fail forward. Failing forward in love means believing that every stumble gets us closer to a love that's right for us.

Loving boldly means risking pain, but it's worth it. Love isn't about never messing up; it's about being willing to learn and grow through each experience.

Fail Forward Together

Relationships are where we learn some of life's biggest lessons. They challenge us, push us, and, yeah, sometimes hurt us. But if we choose to fail forward, each experience becomes part of our journey. We can learn to let go, to welcome vulnerability, and to grow stronger in every connection.

Failing forward in relationships isn't about being perfect or never making mistakes. It's about showing up, learning, and appreciating the journey. Let each connection, whether it lasts or not, help you grow into the person you're meant to be.

So go ahead - fail forward in love, friendship, and family. Let every relationship be part of your journey, helping you find the love, understanding, and connection you deserve.

CHAPTER 5

In Career and Growth

"Success isn't about avoiding setbacks; it's about rising each time, stronger and wiser."

In Career and Growth

Careers - those big dreams we build up, sometimes with expectations piled high. But let's face it: no career path is smooth from start to finish. We get excited about new roles, promotions, projects...only to face rejection, setbacks, or plain old disappointment along the way. Failing forward in your career is about embracing every misstep as a steppingstone, understanding that each "no" or setback is shaping you, preparing you, and moving you closer to where you're meant to be.

Here's the truth: growth in your career doesn't happen because everything goes right. It happens because of the lessons you pick up along the way. When we stop seeing professional setbacks as personal failures and start seeing them as part of the journey, that's when we really start to grow. It's not about the mistakes, it's about what we do with them.

Embracing Rejection as Redirection

Rejection is brutal, especially when you're aiming high. You might get turned down for a job you thought was yours, passed over for a promotion, or receive a "no" on a project you poured everything into. But here's the thing: rejection is often just redirection. It's life's way of saying, "This isn't it, but something else is coming."

Every "no" you encounter is pointing you toward something better aligned with who you are and what you're capable of. When you start looking at rejection this way, you can move forward with less frustration and more curiosity. Instead of asking, "Why didn't I get it?" ask, "What's waiting for me that I can't see yet?"

Learning to Pivot, Not Quit

One of the toughest parts of any career is realizing when it's time to pivot. Maybe you're in a job that doesn't feel right, or a role that's taking more than it's giving. Failing forward doesn't mean you keep pushing in the wrong direction, it means being willing to make a change when something isn't working.

Pivoting doesn't mean giving up. It means being flexible and open to exploring new paths. Each time you pivot, you're not starting over; you're bringing everything you've learned with you. So if something in your career feels like a dead end, don't quit on yourself. Look around, see where you can adjust, and keep moving forward.

Handling Setbacks with Resilience

Setbacks happen. Deadlines get missed, projects fall through, clients cancel, deals don't close. No matter how hard we work, we're bound to face a few falls along the way. Failing forward means letting these setbacks build your resilience instead of letting them knock you down.

Think of every setback as a chance to ask yourself, "What can I take from this experience?" Did you learn a new skill? Did you handle a difficult conversation? Did you uncover a better way to solve a problem? When you shift your focus from what went wrong to what you gained, every setback becomes a win.

Redefining Success and Embracing Imperfection

It's easy to measure success by titles, promotions, or paychecks. But when you're always chasing the next "big win," it's easy to overlook the smaller, everyday victories that really matter. Failing forward in your career is about redefining what success means to you. It's about setting your own standards and remembering that each step forward, no matter how small, is worth celebrating.

Sometimes, success just means showing up and giving your best, even when things are uncertain. Maybe it's taking a risk or stepping out of your comfort zone. Maybe it's trying something new, even if you don't get it perfect the first time. Success isn't about being flawless, it's about being brave enough to keep trying, to keep growing.

Building Connections and Embracing Collaboration

No one achieves career growth alone. Building connections and working with others is key. Yet sometimes relationships at work don't go as planned. You might face conflict, experience misunderstandings, or even deal with betrayal. It happens. But failing forward in your career means using these moments to learn how to build stronger, healthier professional relationships.

Lean into collaboration, even when it's messy. Instead of seeing setbacks with colleagues as failures, see them as lessons in communication, patience, and resilience. Building a career is just as much about building relationships as it is about achieving goals. The people around you can be some of your greatest teachers if you let them.

Turning Disappointments into Fuel

There's no denying that career disappointments can sting. When you've put in the hours and the effort but things still don't go as planned, it's easy to feel defeated. But here's where failing forward really comes into play: use that disappointment as fuel. Let it remind you of what you're working toward and why it matters.

Some of the most successful people in the world faced massive career setbacks. What set them apart was their decision to use those setbacks to work even harder, to innovate, and to keep going when others might have given up. Every disappointment is a reminder of your commitment to yourself and your goals. Use it to push you forward, not pull you down.

Cultivating Patience and Staying the Course

In a world that prizes quick wins, patience can feel like an old-fashioned virtue. But career growth, real growth, takes time. Failing forward means staying the course, even when results don't come overnight. It's about trusting the process and believing that the work you're putting in now will pay off, even if you can't see it yet.

There will be times when it feels like you're moving in slow motion, but remember: slow progress is still progress. The people who make it in their careers aren't always the ones who started with the most talent. They're the ones who didn't give up. Stay patient. Keep pushing. Trust that everything you're doing is leading you exactly where you need to go.

Fail Forward to the Career You Want

Careers aren't built on easy wins. They're built on the lessons, the struggles, and the moments that make you dig deep. Failing forward in your career isn't about getting it right all the time. It's about showing up, learning, and growing through each experience. It's about letting every job, every role, every setback shape you into someone who's stronger, wiser, and more resilient.

Remember, no matter where you are right now, you're moving forward. Each misstep is a part of your journey. Keep going. Keep learning. Keep failing forward. Let each experience push you closer to the career - and the life - you want.

CHAPTER 6

In Health and Wellness

"True wellness is found in the journey, not just the destination. Embrace every stumble as an opportunity to grow stronger and more resilient in body and mind."

In Health and Wellness

Health is personal. We all want to feel our best, but let's be real; wellness is not a straight line. From falling short on our fitness goals to struggling with mental health or dealing with unexpected health issues, the journey to wellness is full of twists, turns, and setbacks. Failing forward in health and wellness means learning from every stumble and understanding that each one can teach us something that'll help us move closer to our goals.

Here's the thing: nobody has it all figured out when it comes to wellness. It's not about achieving perfection. It's about doing what you can, learning from what doesn't work, and showing up for yourself no matter what. Failing forward in health is about making the most of every misstep and keeping our focus on progress, not perfection.

Learning from Physical Setbacks

We've all been there, working toward a fitness goal or just trying to keep up with a workout routine, when something happens. Maybe you got injured, maybe you just lost motivation, or maybe life got busy and your health goals slipped down the list. Physical setbacks happen, but failing forward means taking them in stride. Instead of beating yourself up for falling behind, ask yourself what this experience can teach you. Did you push too hard? Did you skip recovery? Did you lose sight of why you started in the first place?

Every physical setback is a reminder that our bodies need patience and respect. It's okay to rest. It's okay to adjust your goals. Failing forward here means finding balance and being kind to yourself while you figure it out.

Listen to your body, learn from it, and remember that it's never too late to get back on track.

Embracing Wellness as a Journey, Not a Destination

Wellness isn't a box you check off - it's an ongoing journey. We're bombarded with images and messages about what "healthy" should look like, but the truth is, there's no one-size-fits-all approach to wellness. What works for one person might not work for you, and that's okay. Failing forward in wellness means finding what makes you feel good, not what someone else says you should be doing.

Maybe you tried a diet that didn't work for you, or you signed up for a fitness class that you just couldn't get into. Instead of seeing these as failures, look at them as clues. You're learning what works for you and what doesn't. Wellness is a lifelong journey, so there's room to try, adjust, and try again.

Prioritizing Mental Health

Mental health is a huge part of wellness, and sometimes it's the part that gets overlooked the most. We can be so focused on physical goals that we forget how important it is to take care of what's going on inside. Failing forward in mental health means recognizing that struggles are part of the process. It's okay to ask for help. It's okay to have days, weeks, or even months where things don't feel right. Mental health isn't about always feeling good; it's about learning to navigate the times when we don't feel good.

If you've ever felt like you "failed" because you couldn't shake off anxiety, stress, or sadness, remind yourself that these feelings don't define you. Failing forward in mental health means reaching out, seeking support, and giving yourself permission to feel everything without judgment. Sometimes, the biggest act of self-care is allowing yourself to be where you are and knowing that's okay.

Building Healthy Habits One Step at a Time

When it comes to health and wellness, we often think we need to overhaul everything at once. But real, lasting change happens one small step at a time. Maybe you tried going all-in on a new routine, only to burn out a few weeks later. That's not failure, it's just feedback. It's telling you that slow and steady might be the way forward.

Start small. Maybe it's drinking more water, getting outside for a walk, or carving out five minutes to breathe each morning. Each small habit builds momentum, and before you know it, these little steps add up. Failing forward in building healthy habits means recognizing that change doesn't happen overnight. Stick with it, stay consistent, and remember that even the smallest actions make a difference.

Redefining What Progress Looks Like

Progress in health and wellness isn't always visible. Sometimes, it's just about feeling a little better, having a bit more energy, or managing stress in a new way. Failing forward means letting go of rigid expectations and celebrating the wins that don't show up on a scale or in a mirror.

Every time you make a choice that's good for your body or mind, that's progress. Did you get some extra sleep? That's progress. Did you take a break when you needed it? That's progress. Did you choose to move your body, even if it wasn't the hardest workout? That's progress. Every little bit counts, and failing forward in wellness means recognizing that wellness isn't a "look" - it's a feeling.

Letting Go of Perfectionism

In health and wellness, perfectionism is often the enemy of progress. We set high standards for ourselves, and the second we miss a workout, eat something "off plan," or skip a healthy habit, we feel like we've failed. But failing forward means letting go of that all-or-nothing thinking. Wellness is flexible. It's okay to have days when things don't go as planned.

Letting go of perfectionism is about remembering that one "off" day doesn't cancel out all the progress you've made. It's about focusing on consistency, not perfection. Failing forward here means being okay with being human. Show up as best you can and, if you miss a day, pick up where you left off and keep going.

Using Setbacks as Motivation

Health journeys come with plenty of setbacks - whether it's an illness, an injury, or just a lack of motivation. But failing forward means using those setbacks as fuel, not as reasons to quit. Maybe you didn't meet your fitness goal this month, or maybe you had a rough mental health week. Instead of giving up, let it remind you of why you started.

Setbacks can reignite your motivation. They can be a reminder of what you're working toward and why it matters. And the best part? Every time you bounce back, you're proving to yourself that you're stronger than you think.

Failing Forward to a Healthier You

Health and wellness aren't about getting it right every time. They're about showing up for yourself, learning from the journey, and accepting that every step - even the messy ones - brings you closer to feeling your best. Failing forward in wellness means being willing to keep going, even when it's hard, and letting every experience teach you something valuable.

Remember, wellness isn't a destination. It's a series of choices we make every day to honor ourselves. Keep going. Keep learning. Keep failing forward. With every step, you're building a stronger, healthier, and more resilient you.

CHAPTER 7

In Parenting and Family Life

"Family life isn't about getting it right every time; it's about showing up, learning together, and growing through every challenge. Each stumble teaches resilience, patience, and love."

In Parenting and Family Life

Parenting. Family life. It's a whole world of love, laughter, chaos, and - let's be honest - plenty of trial and error. Being a parent or a family member means being there through it all, learning as you go, and picking yourself up after every misstep. We all want to be the perfect role model, to say the right things, to be the steady, loving presence our family needs. But the reality? Sometimes we fall short. Sometimes we mess up. And that's okay.

Failing forward in parenting and family life is about giving yourself permission to grow, make mistakes, and learn right along with the people you love. It's about showing up, doing your best, and knowing that even when things go sideways, there's always a lesson to be learned and a way to move forward.

Embracing Imperfection in Parenting

No parent gets it right every time. Parenting is a constant juggling act, and some days, it feels like you're just trying to keep all the balls in the air. You make mistakes, and guess what? Your kids see it. But here's the silver lining: every mistake is an opportunity to teach your kids something valuable about being human. When you mess up, you're teaching them that it's okay to be imperfect, that everyone makes mistakes, and that it's possible to recover, learn, and keep going.

Failing forward in parenting means giving yourself grace and letting go of the idea that you have to be perfect. Show your kids that it's okay to admit when you're wrong, to apologize, and to make changes. In doing so, you're teaching them one of life's greatest lessons: how to handle setbacks with resilience and self-compassion.

Learning to Listen (Even When It's Hard)

One of the hardest parts of family life is truly listening. Life gets busy, stress builds up, and it's easy to jump to conclusions or react out of frustration. But failing forward as a parent means learning to slow down and really listen to your kids or family members, even when it's tough.

Maybe you didn't respond the way you wanted to, or maybe you got frustrated too quickly. That's okay. Failing forward means taking those moments as reminders to listen better next time. Instead of focusing on where you got it wrong, focus on what you can do differently. Give yourself permission to learn and improve with each conversation.

Setting Boundaries with Love

Boundaries are essential, but they're not always easy to enforce. It's natural to want to say "yes" to your kids or family, to keep everyone happy. But failing forward in parenting sometimes means learning to say "no" for the right reasons. It's about setting limits that protect your time, your energy, and the well-being of everyone involved.

Boundaries teach kids about respect, both for themselves and for others. They show them that love doesn't mean giving in to every demand. When you set boundaries with love, you're teaching them how to respect limits in their own lives. And when you mess up and let those boundaries slide, failing forward means recognizing it, readjusting, and moving forward with a little more balance next time.

Handling Conflicts with Patience

Family life isn't without its conflicts. Arguments happen, misunderstandings occur, and emotions run high. It's easy to let frustration take over, but failing forward means learning to handle these conflicts with patience, even if you don't always get it right.

When you have a disagreement, whether it's with a spouse, a sibling, or a child, remember that every conflict is a chance to model patience and respect. If you slip up, that's okay - failing forward means using each conflict as a learning experience. Talk about what happened, apologize if needed, and let your family see that it's possible to move past disagreements with understanding and kindness.

Showing Up Even When You're Tired

Parenting can be exhausting. Some days, you're running on empty and showing up feels like a struggle. But here's where failing forward can actually help: instead of feeling guilty for not being at your best, remind yourself that just showing up is enough. Even on the tough days, even when you feel like you're barely holding it together, your presence matters more than you know.

Failing forward in these moments means giving yourself credit for being there. It's okay if you're not 100% every single day. Your family doesn't need you to be perfect - they just need you to show up. When you're honest about your limitations, you're showing them what it means to keep going, even when things aren't easy.

Embracing Growth Together

Every family is a work in progress. Just like individuals, families grow, adapt, and change over time. Failing forward means embracing this growth as a family, being willing to try new things, and allowing each other to make mistakes along the way.

If something didn't go as planned - a family trip that went off the rails, a household project that didn't turn out right - let it be a lesson. Laugh about it together, talk about what you'd do differently, and let each misstep become part of the story. Failing forward as a family means letting go of the need for perfection and choosing to grow together instead.

Letting Go of Control

One of the toughest parts of parenting is realizing that you can't control everything. Kids have minds of their own, and sometimes they'll make choices you don't agree with. But failing forward means learning to let go, trusting that they'll find their own way, and supporting them as they do.

When you let go of control, you're giving your kids the freedom to explore, to learn from their own mistakes, and to become resilient. You're showing them that life isn't about following a set path but about discovering who they are and what matters to them. Failing forward here is about embracing the unpredictability of family life and trusting that, no matter what, love will guide the way.

Failing Forward as a Family

Parenting and family life present some of the most meaningful - and challenging - experiences we'll ever have. And the truth is, there's no perfect formula. Failing forward as a parent or family member means being willing to learn, to apologize, to adjust, and to keep showing up with love.

Remember, family life isn't about getting it right all the time. It's about building a foundation of love, support, and growth. Each mistake, each misunderstanding, each apology, they're all part of the journey. And with every moment, you're teaching your family that love isn't about perfection. It's about presence, resilience, and the courage to keep going, together.

So keep going. Keep learning. Keep failing forward. Because every step, every lesson, every moment of growth brings you closer to the kind of family you're working to build - a family that's strong, loving, and unafraid to embrace life's imperfections, together.

CHAPTER 8

Through Financial Setbacks

"Financial setbacks are tough, but they're also teachers. Being broke builds resilience, teaches humility, and prepares you for a stronger future. Every setback is just a setup for a powerful comeback."

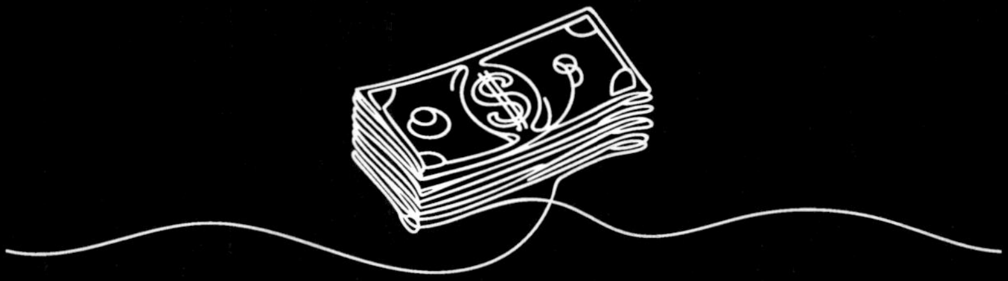

Through Financial Setbacks

Financial struggles can shake you to your core. Money problems don't just affect your wallet; they affect your mind, your spirit, and your sense of security. I know because I've been there. I've been at rock bottom financially, in ways that most people would never guess. In 2012, during one of the darkest times of my life, I went through a terrible divorce that left me spinning. For three months, I struggled just to keep a roof over my head. Homeless and staying in and out of hotels, I was barely holding on, all while working a six-figure job and living with a credit score of 480. It felt like life had pulled the rug out from under me, leaving me raw, exposed, and wondering how I'd ever climb out.

But here's what I learned: financial setbacks don't define you. They don't determine your worth or limit your future. Failing forward financially means accepting the tough moments as part of your story, using them to grow stronger, and finding ways to rebuild, even when you're starting from ground zero. Financial setbacks can feel impossible to overcome, but with resilience and the right mindset, you can take every tough moment and turn it into a steppingstone toward a more secure future.

Facing Rock Bottom

There's something humbling about hitting rock bottom. For me, it was the experience of working a well-paying job and still not having a stable place to sleep at night. It was a kind of financial isolation. On paper, it looked like I was doing fine, but in reality, I was scrambling. And that's the thing about financial hardship - it's often invisible to others. You carry it quietly, sometimes feeling ashamed, sometimes wondering if you'll ever find your footing again.

Failing forward from rock bottom means recognizing that everyone's journey has low points. You're not alone, even if it feels that way. Acknowledging where you are is the first step to moving forward. Once you're honest about your situation, you can start making decisions that help you, not ones driven by fear or desperation.

Letting Go of Shame and Self-Blame

Financial setbacks come with a lot of emotional weight. It's easy to fall into a loop of shame and self-blame, wondering what you could have done differently. For me, it was a constant tug-of-war between pride and pain. I'd built a career, achieved a certain level of success, and then it all felt like it had slipped away. But here's the truth: shame holds you back from growth. Letting go of shame and accepting that financial setbacks happen - even to those who work hard and "do everything right" - is essential to moving forward.

Failing forward financially is about giving yourself grace. Financial hardship doesn't mean you're irresponsible or unworthy. It means you're human. Let go of the shame, and make room for a plan to move ahead.

Building a New Foundation

After my time in and out of hotels, with a credit score that felt like it was dragging me down, I knew I needed a fresh start. Rebuilding from financial setbacks is a process, and it doesn't happen overnight. For me, it started with small, intentional changes - making a budget, setting aside whatever I could, and finding ways to improve my credit score little by little. It was humbling but also empowering. I learned that when you focus on building small habits, they add up over time.

If you're struggling financially, start by creating a foundation, no matter how small it seems. Maybe it's setting up a savings account, working on a debt repayment plan, or learning how to track your spending. Each small step forward is a brick in the new foundation you're building.

Navigating Financial Stress

Financial stress is like a weight that follows you everywhere. It affects your mood, your sleep, and your relationships. During those months, I remember the constant stress - worrying about where I'd sleep, if I'd be able to pay for another night at a hotel, and what my future looked like. The pressure was constant. But I learned that when you're in survival mode, you have to take it day by day. Focus on what you can control, even if it's just one small thing at a time.

Failing forward in financial stress means finding ways to manage your mental health and stay grounded. Whether it's through journaling, talking to someone you trust, or taking breaks to breathe, managing stress is key. Financial setbacks can feel overwhelming, but they don't have to consume you. Small moments of relief add up, helping you stay strong for the journey ahead.

Rebuilding Credit and Financial Confidence

With a credit score of 480, I knew I had a long road ahead. Every time I applied for something or checked my credit report, it was a reminder of where I was. But failing forward means learning from each setback, using every mistake as a guide for the future. I started paying off small debts, setting up auto-payments to avoid missing bills, and slowly my credit score began to inch up. It wasn't a fast process, but with each small win, I started to regain my confidence.

If you're rebuilding financially, take it one step at a time. Don't focus on the big picture all at once. Just focus on what you can do today, then tomorrow, and keep moving forward. Remember, each positive step adds up, and even small improvements can build momentum.

Moving From Survival to Stability

During that period, I was in survival mode, just trying to get by. But as I took steps to rebuild, I started to shift from survival to stability. Failing forward financially means recognizing that stability takes time. It's not about rushing to get back to where you were but instead building a sustainable foundation that supports your well-being in the long term.

As you start to move out of survival mode, set small goals. Maybe it's saving $50 a month or paying down one credit card. Each step toward stability gives you more security and peace of mind. It's not about perfection; it's about progress.

Giving Yourself Credit for the Journey

Financial setbacks can feel like failures, but they're often just part of the journey. For me, those months of struggle and uncertainty taught me resilience in ways nothing else could. I learned that my worth isn't tied to my bank account or my credit score. I learned that I could rebuild, even from rock bottom, and that every challenge taught me a new level of strength.

Failing forward financially means giving yourself credit for what you've been through. It's about recognizing that financial success isn't a straight line, and setbacks are just steppingstones on your way to something better.

Failing Forward Toward Financial Freedom

Financial setbacks can feel like they're going to define your whole life, but they don't have to. Failing forward means learning from each struggle, taking it one step at a time, and remembering that even the toughest times don't last forever. If you're going through financial hardship, know that you're not alone. It's possible to rebuild, to move from survival to stability, and to find freedom on the other side.

Remember, financial success isn't about never making mistakes. It's about learning from them, growing stronger, and refusing to let them hold you back. Keep going. Keep learning. Keep failing forward. Because each step you take is leading you to a more secure, more fulfilling future.

CHAPTER 9

In Community and Social Impact

"True impact isn't about instant results; it's about showing up, learning from setbacks, and staying committed to change. Every small action builds toward a brighter, stronger community."

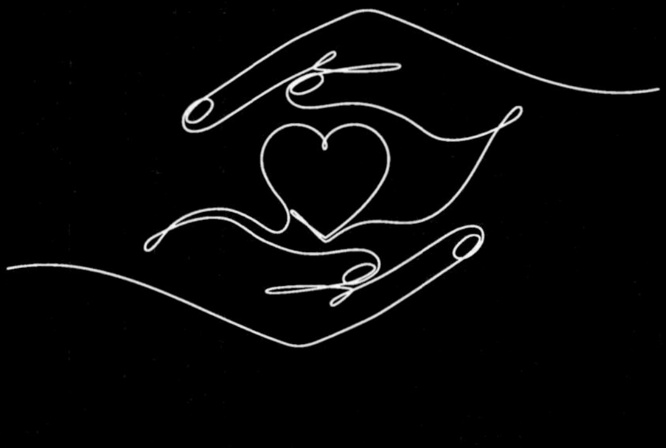

In Community and Social Impact

Most of us want to make a difference, to leave a positive mark on the world, and to help others find their way when times are tough. For me, this dream is personal. One day, I want to build a container home park - a place where people who've fallen on hard times, those struggling with homelessness, addiction, or just life itself, can find a safe, warm place to live. A place where they're not just given shelter but real support. My goal is to help them restart their lives, shift their mindsets, and rediscover what it means to contribute, to feel valued, and to have hope.

Big dreams like these aren't achieved overnight, and the path to creating real community change is rarely smooth. There are moments of frustration, times when plans fall through, and setbacks that make you question whether you're making any impact at all. But failing forward in community and social impact work means seeing each stumble, each detour, as part of the journey. Real change takes time, persistence, and the willingness to keep showing up - even when things don't go as planned.

Starting Small and Building Momentum

People often think making a difference requires big actions, but meaningful change almost always starts small. Failing forward here means letting go of the pressure to start with the "perfect" plan and instead just taking one small step at a time. Maybe that's volunteering, donating resources, or organizing a small community event. When you start small, you're building a foundation that can grow over time. Each effort, no matter how small, builds momentum and helps you learn what works and what doesn't.

Every conversation you have, every time you show up to help, you're adding to the impact. Failing forward means understanding that every small action counts, even if it doesn't feel like much right now. Step by step, you're laying the groundwork to make those bigger dreams a reality.

Learning Through Rejection and Resistance

When you're working toward a big vision, you'll likely face resistance. People may doubt your goals, turn down your ideas, or question your methods. You might propose a project only to have it rejected, or try to rally people around a cause and find they're not interested. Failing forward in these moments means recognizing that people often resist change because they're unsure or uncomfortable. It doesn't mean your vision is wrong.

Each "no" or moment of pushback is an opportunity to adjust your approach, refine your message, and keep pushing forward. Instead of letting rejection stop you, use it to build resilience. Remember, creating real change requires patience and the courage to keep going, even when others don't see the potential yet.

Embracing Collaboration, Even When It's Messy

Creating community impact usually involves working with others, and collaboration can be a challenge. Different personalities, ideas, and goals can create tension. But failing forward means learning to see these challenges as chances to grow stronger together. Community impact isn't something you do alone. It's something built through shared vision and collective effort.

When collaboration gets messy, remind yourself that each experience teaches you something about working with others, finding common ground, and navigating differences. With patience, openness, and a commitment to the bigger goal, you can build a stronger, more sustainable impact.

Staying Resilient in the Face of Setbacks

Setbacks are inevitable when you're working toward something meaningful. Plans might fall apart, resources can dry up, and events might not turn out the way you'd hoped. Failing forward here means using these setbacks to build resilience. Ask yourself, "What can I learn from this?" Maybe it's a lesson in preparation, a chance to pivot, or an opportunity to refine your approach.

Every setback is a chance to grow tougher, to adapt, and to come back stronger. Remember, lasting impact isn't built in a day. It takes time, resilience, and a commitment to keep showing up for your vision.

Celebrating the Small Wins

In the pursuit of big dreams, it's easy to overlook the small victories along the way. But failing forward means taking the time to celebrate each small win. Did a few extra people show up to help? That's a win. Did someone you helped tell you their life feels just a little better because of your work? That's a win, too.

Every small success is proof that you're on the right path. These small moments are what fuel your progress and remind you why you started. Failing forward in social impact means recognizing that every small step matters, even when you're aiming for something big.

Making Space for Reflection and Self-Care

Community work can take a toll on your energy, your time, and sometimes even your health. It's easy to pour everything into the mission, especially when it's something you're deeply passionate about. But failing forward means understanding that you can't help others if you're running on empty. Make time to step back, reflect, and recharge.

Self-care isn't selfish. It's necessary. Taking time to reflect on your journey, celebrate progress, and rest ensures that you can keep showing up fully present and committed to the cause. By taking care of yourself, you're setting a foundation for sustainable impact.

Accepting That You Can't Change Everything

One of the hardest parts of community work is accepting that you can't solve every problem. There will be people you can't reach, issues you can't fix, and situations that are beyond your control. Failing forward here means focusing on what you can do and letting go of the rest.

Your impact might not solve every problem, but it's still meaningful. Each person you help, each action you take, adds up to something bigger. Failing forward means recognizing that your efforts are part of a larger movement toward change, even if you don't see immediate results.

Failing Forward to Build a Better World

Creating a meaningful impact in the world isn't easy, but it's worth it. For me, the vision of a container home park - a place where people struggling with homelessness, addiction, or tough times can find a fresh start - is what keeps me going. It's a big goal, and I know the road won't be easy. But I also know that every setback, every lesson, and every small win is part of getting there.

Failing forward in community and social impact means embracing each obstacle, celebrating progress, and staying committed to your vision. Remember, real change is built over time, through resilience, persistence, and a willingness to learn along the way. Keep pushing, keep learning, and keep showing up, because every step, no matter how small, brings you closer to making that dream a reality.

So, fail forward with courage. Stay focused on your mission, welcome the journey, and know that each small action adds up. Together, we can build a future where everyone has a chance to rebuild, to grow, and to find hope. Your journey, your impact, and your dream matter. And with each step forward, you're making the world a better place.

CHAPTER 10

Preparing For the Journey Ahead

"The journey won't be easy, but each step makes you stronger. Embrace the challenges - they're all part of your growth."

Preparing For the Journey Ahead

Remember, failure doesn't define us, it's how we respond that shapes our path. The journey of failing forward isn't about perfection or breezing through life without setbacks. It's about embracing the messiness of growth, learning from every fall, and finding the strength to keep moving forward. Since that morning in 2009, I've learned that every setback holds a lesson, and every failure carries the seeds of success if we're willing to see it that way.

The path ahead won't always be smooth. Some days, you'll stumble; other days, it might feel like you're moving in reverse. That's all part of the process. The next 100 pages are filled with insights and motivational quotes to keep you grounded and inspired when things get tough. Think of each quote as fuel for your journey - reminders that failure isn't the opposite of success but a necessary step on the path toward it.

These quotes are more than just words - they're guideposts, little sparks of wisdom that have lifted me through challenging times and reminded me to keep going. And now, they're here for you, too. Use them as anchors when doubt tries to pull you down. Let them remind you that falling isn't final, what matters is that we rise, learn, and keep pushing forward. Let these quotes inspire you to fail boldly, knowing that every misstep brings you closer to the person you're meant to become.

Imagine each quote as a daily ritual, a reminder to carry with you for the next 100 days. Research shows that doing something for 100 days can profoundly change us. Our brains are adaptable, and repeating an action, like reflecting on these quotes, can reshape the way we think and respond. By revisiting these reminders each day, you're creating new neural pathways and strengthening your commitment to this mindset.

Committing to this journey for 100 days will also reinforce your motivation, thanks to dopamine, the "feel-good" chemical our brain releases when we experience something positive. That burst of dopamine can encourage you to keep going, helping build momentum with each day you invest in this mindset. And as the days add up, this daily practice will become a habit, a natural part of who you are.

Taking on a 100-day journey like this can transform the way you see yourself. Each day you engage with these quotes, you're proving to yourself that you're capable of consistency and commitment, which strengthens your confidence in achieving your goals. Even small daily moments of reflection build self-discipline and instill a growth mindset, encouraging you to see challenges as chances to learn and grow.

Of course, everyone's path is different, and building a habit may take more or less time depending on the individual. The most important factor is consistency, just showing up, even if it's only for a moment. If the quotes resonate with you, take that as a sign to keep going. By dedicating this time each day, even in small doses, you're laying a strong foundation for lasting change. And if any challenge feels overwhelming, start small. Progress, even gradual, is still progress.

This is the essence of the fail forward mentality: to focus on progress over perfection, resilience over regret, and to keep moving forward, one step at a time. Now, let's dive into the words that have carried me forward, in the hope that they'll inspire you to create your own path, one day and one quote at a time.

Here's to your journey of resilience, courage, and transformation. The pages ahead are filled with powerful quotes that have carried me through my own setbacks and helped me find strength in moments of doubt. Each quote is a spark, a reminder that failure is not the end but an essential part of growth. These words are here to guide you, especially when the path feels uncertain. They're here to lift you up, remind you of your own power, and reignite that belief in yourself when you need it most.

As you immerse yourself in these quotes, let them become more than just words on a page. Let them settle deep within you, shaping the way you see challenges and reframing how you define success. Each quote is an invitation to pause, reflect, and reset. They'll help you remember that every stumble is an opportunity, every obstacle a chance to build something stronger within yourself. By the end, you may find yourself viewing the world differently, seeing challenges not as setbacks but as steppingstones, learning to use failure as fuel for growth.

Imagine the possibilities if, each day, these words were to guide you to face life's ups and downs with a little more courage, a little more resilience, and a lot more hope. Imagine how your world could change if you carried this fail forward mentality through every moment of self-doubt and uncertainty. These quotes are here to anchor you in that mindset, to remind you that strength isn't just about winning but about how you rise after every fall.

With each quote you read, may your mindset grow stronger, your spirit feel lighter, and your resolve deepen. This journey is yours to take on, and by the end, you'll see that you've become someone who faces life head-on, unafraid of challenges and unshaken by setbacks. Here's to a new chapter, one fueled by purpose, resilience, and a commitment to failing forward. Let these quotes be your guide and get ready to see just how powerful you truly are.

CHAPTER 11

100 Motivational Quotes

“Consistency over time builds the foundation for success. Small, steady steps achieve more than a single leap.”

"Speak what you seek until you see what you've said."

One of my favorite quotes is by Chris Gardner, whose story inspired *The Pursuit of Happyness*. His journey resonates deeply with me. I believe the words we speak shape what we believe, what we act on, and ultimately what we expect to happen. And often, what we expect to happen *does* happen in the end. There's immense power in what we speak.

Fail forward.

“Don’t be the only thing standing in your way.”

Sometimes we, ourselves, are the only thing stopping us from the progress we want to make in our lives, our careers, and even our relationships. If this is you, get out of your own way and allow yourself to be great. You deserve it.

Fail forward.

"Be good to people."

It costs $0.00 to be kind, but the ROI for being good to people is infinite.

Fail forward.

“Joy is what happens when we allow ourselves to recognize how good things really are.”

Take some time to stop and take inventory of how blessed you really are. You are alive, you are breathing, you are here. Find joy today.

Fail forward.

"Small wins add up."

You are building momentum every time you win, big or small. Even your small wins add up over time. An empire isn't built in a day but one brick at a time. Don't forget to celebrate along the way!

Fail forward.

“Your past doesn’t need you anymore, your future does.”

What’s behind you is behind you. Focus all your focus, forward.

Fail forward.

"There are 7 days in a week and someday isn't one of them."

Whatever you keep putting off will continue staring you in the face until you take action. Make "someday" today!

Fail forward.

“A beautiful day begins with a beautiful mindset.”

Your thoughts shape your outcome. It’s that simple. Start each day with positive thoughts, and you set the stage for a positive experience. Begin with doubt, and it colors your day; focus on the good, and everything shifts. Your mindset matters more than you know. Each day is a choice in how you show up, so choose wisely.

Fail forward.

"Every storm runs out of rain."

I can remember when life felt so heavy and almost unbearable. I never thought I'd get out or even be able to breathe again. Let me tell you, nothing lasts forever. If you are going through a storm, keep going. The rain eventually stops, the sun comes back out, and that's when you bloom.

Fail forward.

“Be the kind of energy you want to attract.”

This quote resonates with me because it’s simple but powerful: the energy you put out is what you get back. Positivity and confidence attract the same in return, while negativity also draws more of the same. Think about people who inspire you - they radiate resilience and confidence. Bring that energy, and you’ll attract the right people and opportunities. Life will knock you down, but the way you rise makes all the difference.

Fail forward.

"Visualization is daydreaming with a purpose."

When I was young my mom would tell me to lay on my back, close my eyes and visualize myself scoring a touchdown, hitting a homerun, clearing the high jump bar. Once the opportunity came, I'd already done it successfully in my mind, therefore it felt more possible in reality. I still do this in daily life. Visualize success before it happens.

Fail forward.

“Be brave enough to suck at something new.”

Often, we allow the fear of failure to stop us from ever trying something new. Here’s the reality: you are probably going to suck at first. That’s okay, just start. While others may laugh when you fall, remember you are stumbling to greatness, and they will have to watch.

Fail forward.

"The longer you stay in your comfort zone, the longer you will feel uncomfortable."

Comfort zones become coffins. The longer you stay in your comfort zone, the more complacent you will become. It's time to move.

Fail forward.

"Never beg for a seat at the table when you can build your own table."

When you find yourself feeling undervalued, overlooked and underappreciated, it's probably time to build your own table.

Fail forward.

“Once you become fearless, life becomes limitless.”

The moment you are able to push past fear, the possibilities are endless.

Fail forward.

“Breathe.”

Take some time today to pause, clear your thoughts and focus on your breathing. Be in the moment. Be present. Just breathe. You’re doing great.

Fail forward.

"Everything you want wants you more."

Whatever you are seeking is also seeking you. Keep a positive mindset, continue your pursuit with diligence, and you will run right into what is running toward you.

Fail forward.

“You either quit or keep going. They both hurt.”

In the end, we will only regret the chances we didn’t take. If you think it’s hard now, wait until you see how hard regret feels.

Fail forward.

"Be realistic and expect a miracle."

Miracles happen every single day. Expecting miracles to happen is not unrealistic. Besides, you are a miracle yourself.

Fail forward.

"The goal isn't to take lots of vacations, it's to create a life you don't need a vacation from."

Let's be honest, everyone loves a good vacation. But what if every day felt like one? Life shouldn't be about working a job until you are drained to the point where you need a vacation. Instead, seek a life where you don't need a vacation but rather are allowed to enjoy one.

Fail forward.

"It's not too late."

People often hold back on their dreams, thinking it's too late. But it's not.

Consider this: Samuel L. Jackson's first big role was at 46, Stan Lee published his first major comic at 40, Morgan Freeman broke through in film at 52, and Louise Bourgeois gained fame as an artist at 78.

It's never too late.

Fail forward.

"Learn to turn your pain into power and your wounds into wisdom."

The things we go through in this life aren't for naught. The pain you endure will become your power, and your wounds will become wisdom.

Fail forward.

"Truth lives in action."

You can always tell what someone believes by the actions they take. You've heard the saying "actions speak louder than words." Actions equal truth. What's your truth? Take action.

Fail forward.

"Focus your focus."

Distractions are everywhere, and it's pretty easy to lose focus on your goals. Most of the time, it's because we are trying to focus on too much at once. Eliminate the things that aren't helping you achieve your primary goal.

Fail forward.

"Good energy is contagious."

Be sure you are bringing good energy into every room, situation, and/or discussion. You have the power to shift the dynamics in the atmosphere. Bring it!

Fail forward.

“Never allow what’s meant to be a sentence to become a chapter in your life.”

From beginning to end, our lives are a story. Recognize the difference between a moment and a milestone. Never let a bad day make you feel like you have a bad life.

Fail forward.

"If you can see it in your mind, you can hold it in your hand."

Our realities begin in our minds. If you can think it, you can have it.

Fail forward.

“You don’t need their approval.”

For years and years, I sought the approval of others. Approval to switch jobs, start a business, have a relationship, leave a relationship, to lose weight, to gain weight, to buy a house, to rent a house, to invest, to live the life I wanted. What I learned is that no matter what I did, the approval never came. Stop this today. You don’t need their approval. Just live.

Fail forward.

"The only way out is through."

Sometimes you will not be able to get around it. You can't go over or under it. You are going to have to face it head on, and just go through. I promise you will be much stronger on the other side.

Fail forward.

“Create the things you wish existed.”

If it hasn't been done yet, maybe the universe is waiting on you to create it.

Fail forward.

"Your attitude before activity will determine your achievement."

The great Henry Ford said, "Whether you think you can or think you can't, you're right." This couldn't be a truer statement. If you go into something with a poor attitude, expect poor results. If you go into something with a great attitude, expect great results.

Fail forward.

"Just start."

This is your sign. You know what to do.

Fail forward.

"Slow progress is still forward progress."

Imagine where you will be 6 months from now if you start slow today. Any amount of forward progress is more than none. Start slowly and gain momentum over time. Then fly!

Fail forward.

"You attract what you're ready for."

The opportunities in life only come when we are ready to seize them. You're ready, now own it.

Fail forward.

"Pay attention to who you are with when you feel your best."

The people we surround ourselves with matter. When you feel most alive, take inventory of who is with you. They are your tribe.

Fail forward.

“Why not you?”

One of my favorite college coaches, Joe Danna, always asked, “Why not you?” Why not you to make the big play, the big catch, the ESPN highlight? This question stuck with me and drives me every day. It’s one of the reasons I’ve come this far, because I believe it can be me. So, I’ll ask you: why not you? Why not you for the big promotion, the big client, the award, or starting your own business? Why not you?

Thanks, Coach!

Fail forward.

"Educate to elevate, not to intimidate."

One of the worst things you can do is use your wisdom to make someone else feel small. When you are providing advice or teaching someone something, do it in a way that elevates them and their knowledge instead of intimidating them with yours.

Fail forward.

“Your attitude in the hallway determines what kind of door will open for you.”

They say when one door closes, another one opens. How your attitude is during the time between is what dictates your next opportunity. Be sure it’s a positive one.

Fail forward.

"Start replacing 'I have to' with 'I get to' and watch your life change."

Perspective is everything! Instead of saying, "I have to go to work on Monday" replace it with "I get to go to work on Monday." The more you see life's events as opportunities instead of hurdles, the smoother your ride will be.

Fail forward.

“Wait until you see why God made you wait.”

When you look back on your life and all the times you had to be patient for something, it all makes sense. Whether it be a job, a degree, a promotion or even marriage, sometimes waiting works out for the best. Often, you don’t realize it until later. Be patient and trust the process.

Fail forward.

"Unsubscribe."

I finally did something that made me incredibly happy - I unsubscribed from a daily email that had annoyed me for months. It felt so good, a real sense of relief. You're probably thinking, "Why not sooner?" The truth is, we all let little annoyances linger instead of addressing them. Start removing small irritations from your life so you can focus on what truly matters. Unsubscribe from anything that no longer adds value.

You'll thank yourself later.

Fail forward.

“Scars mean you’re alive.”

Never allow a scar to make you feel shame. Scars mean you were stronger than whatever tried to harm you. Let that be a reminder. You are strong, you are a survivor, and you are alive.

Fail forward.

“Keep showing up.”

Daily. Attending every lecture in college would get you a “C.” Sometimes, half the battle is just showing up. Start there, the rest will happen how it should. Your presence is needed.

Fail forward.

"Being wanted feeds the ego. Being valued feeds the soul."

There is a huge difference between being wanted and being valued. Feeding one's ego is only temporary. Feeding the soul lasts forever. Be where you are valued.

Fail forward.

"Stop making excuses for your excuses."

There comes a point in life where you are faced with your own self. You either get tired of hearing your own excuses, or you will continue to make excuses for your own mediocrity. Own up - you deserve better, and you know it.

Fail forward.

“Triggers mean you haven’t healed.”

We all have triggers. These are things that remind us of something that may have hurt us in one way or another. When we haven’t addressed those issues, forgiven, and truly moved on with life, that is when those reminders trigger us. This means you haven’t healed.

It’s time you healed.

Fail forward.

"Even when it feels uncomfortable, grow."

Imagine how the rose feels breaking through soil, pressing past thorns, to reach the sunlight. Growth is never a comfortable process, but it is necessary.

Fail forward.

“The moment you realize your worth, it increases.”

Many people walk this earth without realizing just how amazing they truly are. Their gifts, talents and abilities have been overlooked for so long, they don’t even realize their worth. The moment they do, it will instantly increase.

Fail forward.

"Character is what you have left when you lose everything you can lose."

They say you learn a lot about yourself when you have everything and when you have nothing. I believe that you learn the most about yourself when you are down to nothing. That's when your true character comes out. Pay attention to who you are when you lose.

Fail forward.

“Hustle until the people you couldn’t reach, start reaching out to you.”

When you focus on your goals and put in the work, your progress becomes undeniable, and those who once overlooked you will see your value. Success has a way of drawing attention, and your persistence will turn the tables in your favor.--

Fail forward.

"Find balance."

At 26, I left a job because I thought I was underpaid, a decision I now see as short-sighted. That job offered priceless benefits: chef-cooked lunches, creative freedom, skill-building opportunities, hiring power, a spacious office, and remarkable flexibility. Young friends, remember, "the grass isn't always greener on the other side," and if it looks greener, the water bill is probably higher.

Life and career shouldn't always be about money - find balance.

Fail forward.

"The sky is not the limit, your mind is."

Stop limiting yourself, your abilities and your potential by what you think about yourself. Your mind is the only limit. Break through that ceiling of thought. Be limitless.

Fail forward.

"Faith and fear cannot coexist."

You cannot have faith that something will happen for you while also fearing it won't. They cancel each other out. Either have faith or doubt, but not both. You choose.

Fail forward.

"Difficult is not the same as impossible."

There will be a lot of things in life that feel difficult to achieve, overcome or get through. This doesn't mean they're impossible. The task may seem impossible until it's finished. Push through.

Fail forward.

"Fly higher."

The only bird that will dare peck at an eagle is the crow. The crow sits on the eagle's back and bites his neck. The eagle does not respond or even fight with the crow. It simply opens its wings and begins to rise higher and higher in the sky. The higher the eagle flies, the harder it is for the crow to breathe. Due to a lack of oxygen, the crow falls away and the eagle is free.

The moral of the story: stop wasting your time worrying about crows.

Just fly higher.

Fail forward.

“Be you, they’ll adjust.”

Stop changing yourself for people who like you better as yourself anyway. Be yourself.

Fail forward.

"Allow yourself to receive."

I've heard many people say they don't take compliments well. Why not? Do they not believe they deserve to be complimented? To feel good about themselves for a moment? To be acknowledged, noticed, seen? Everyone deserves to receive good things in life. Be grateful, accept it, and pass it on.

Fail forward.

"A gentle hand can shake the whole world."

There is much more power in kindness than we give it credit for. Kindness has the ability to change the world, even if it's only someone's world. Be gentle.

Fail forward.

"Take your dreams seriously."

You have dreams for a reason. When they come to you, it's a preview of what is to come. Believe that your dreams are possible.

Fail forward.

“You either quit or keep going. They both hurt.”

Read that again.

Fail forward.

“Stop monitoring things you left in God’s hands.”

We often are what stops us from receiving the things we leave in God’s hands, because we still feel the need to “help” God. God doesn’t need our help. If you prayed about it and placed it in His hands, get out of the way, have faith, and get ready for the blessing.

Fail forward.

“Have you tried praying about it as much as you’ve been worrying about it?”

Pray about it and then get some rest tonight.

Fail forward.

"If you were able to believe in Santa Claus for 8 years, you can believe in yourself for 5 minutes."

Enough said.

Fail forward.

“Expect great things.”

Our expectations shape our reality. Start expecting great things instead of thinking, "It will always be this way."

When I get an email or a call, I expect it to bring great news or an amazing opportunity. Each morning, I expect it to be a great day. You’ll be amazed at how life shifts when you change the way you see it.

Expect great things, and great things will find you.

Fail forward.

"Long story, short – it all works out."

It does. It always does.

Fail forward.

“Plan for abundance, not for shortage.”

Whatever you focus on, grows.

Fail forward.

"Who you were, who you are, and who you will become are three different mindsets."

Same person, different mindset.

Fail forward.

"Your worth is not up for debate."

Stop allowing others to determine your worth. It's not up for debate.

Fail forward.

“High-vibe magic can’t happen in low-vibe places.”

Sometimes your surroundings are stopping your growth.

Fail forward.

“Imperfect action is better than perfect inaction.”

Be brave enough to fail and learn.

Fail forward.

"Embrace the process."

If you feel trapped or overwhelmed, think of the caterpillar before it becomes a butterfly. Embrace the process. This is just a season, and it will pass. Soon, you'll soar more beautiful than ever!

Fail forward.

“You aren’t owed anything.”

“What you want in life, you need to work for and earn!" - My dad

Fail forward.

"The next level will require you to let people go instead of proving your worth to them."

At some point you have to move on. It's now.

Fail forward.

“Extraordinary magic is woven through ordinary life.”

Just take a look around you.

Fail forward.

"Stop ducking to fit under ceilings that other people have set for you."

Stand tall.

Fail forward.

"Overnight success?"

No such thing.

Sylvester Stallone sold his dog to survive before Rocky. J.K. Rowling faced 12 rejections before *Harry Potter* saw the light. Walt Disney was fired for "lacking imagination," and Steve Jobs was ousted from his own company. Behind every big win is a story of resilience, late nights, and relentless perseverance.

There is no such thing as an overnight success. Success takes hard work, long nights, rejection, failure, perseverance, and grit.

Fail forward.

"If you don't come from a rich family, a rich family must come from you."

This is not about money.

Fail forward.

“When you face your fears, you are also forcing your fears to face you.”

Trust me, they don’t want to see you.

Fail forward.

“Rare breed.”

There is a rare breed of people that go all in. They keep their word. They give it all. They go the extra mile for those they care for. These individuals hardly ever receive the same passion and effort in return, yet never change and always give their all. To the givers, forgivers, and selfless lovers out there - keep being beautiful.

Don’t let this cold world change you and take advantage of every little moment you are given.

Fail forward.

“If you’ve lost someone but found yourself, you’ve won.”

Read that again.

Fail forward.

“God did.”

In case you're wondering how I did it - I didn't.

God did.

In case you're wondering how I'm doing it - I'm not.

God is.

In case you're wondering how I will do it - I won't.

God will.

Fail forward.

“Your vision for your life is possible, that’s why you have it.”

The visions we have in our lives are simply teasers for what is to come.

Fail forward.

“Lay a solid foundation with the bricks that others have thrown at you.”

And stack them neatly.

Fail forward.

“Growing may feel like breaking at first.”

This is why they are called growing pains. If it hurts, you’re going the right way.

Fail forward.

"A lion does not wake up and decide to be a gazelle for the day."

Hunt, stop just surviving.

Fail forward.

“Remember why you started.”

When it becomes too hard to continue, remember why you started. When it doesn't feel worth it anymore, remember why you started. When you've been rejected over and over, remember why you started. When you've run out of money, remember why you started. When everyone else tells you to quit, remember why you started. When you get tired of failing, remember why you started.

Then fail again.

Fail forward.

"Watch your thoughts."

It's easy to spot a yellow car when you're always thinking of a yellow car.

It's easy to spot an opportunity when you're always thinking of an opportunity.

It's easy to be mad when you're always thinking of being mad.

You become what you constantly think about.

Watch your thoughts.

Fail forward.

“Every winner is just a loser who tried one more time.”

The power of one more.

Fail forward.

"A healthy man wants a thousand things, a sick man only wants one."

Read that again.

Fail forward.

“Be a doer.”

In life, there are doers and talkers. While the doers are doing, the talkers are talking. The doers do what the talkers talk about doing, yet never do. The talkers talk about the doers for doing, while the doers get stuff done. The doers only talk once they've done what the talkers talked about doing, yet never did.

Be a doer.

Fail forward.

“The comeback is personal, it’s an apology to myself.”

Make is personal. You owe you.

Fail forward.

“Stop letting your mind create problems that do not exist.”

Read that again.

Fail forward.

"Just because it's taking time doesn't mean it's not happening."

There is so much power in patience.

We live in a world that's always rushing, always pushing for the next thing. But real growth, real change? It takes time. When you learn to wait, to trust the process, you start to see things differently. Patience isn't about doing nothing, it's about understanding that everything happens when it's supposed to.

Don't rush your journey. Let it unfold.

Fail forward.

“You will never find your worth in the same place that made you question it.”

Read that again, then move on.

Fail forward.

“You are not alive just to survive.

Wake up and be great.

It’s a simple choice you make every morning. You decide how you’ll show up in the world. You can let the day happen to you, or you can own it, step up, and be the best version of yourself. Greatness doesn’t just happen, it’s something you commit to, day in and day out.

So, start your day with that mindset. Be intentional. Be great.

Fail forward.

“What they thought was your peak was actually your launching pad.”

It’s time for takeoff!

Fail forward.

"No pressure, no diamonds."

At 30, I was in one of the lowest places of my life, feeling miserable, lonely, and defeated. The weight of the world was crushing me. Then one morning, I read a quote that changed everything: "Pressure can burst pipes, but it also creates diamonds." From that moment, I welcomed the hard times, knowing they were shaping me. No pressure, no diamonds.

Fail forward.

"The best part of being authentic is there is no image to maintain."

You just have to be yourself.

Fail forward.

"Those who conquer the fear of rejection become unstoppable."

Fear is an illusion and rejection is merely redirection. The sooner you come to this understanding, the sooner you become unstoppable.

Fail forward.

"Be where your feet are."

Be present. Be in the moment. Be grateful. Be centered. Be where your feet are.

Fail forward.

Acknowledgements

First and foremost, I have to extend my deepest gratitude to my rock and the love of my life, Kim. Your unwavering support, endless love, and constant patience have been my pillars, holding me up through the highs and lows that came along this journey. I am eternally grateful for the unconditional love and understanding you've created for us.

To my wonderful children, Cayden, Connor, Noah, and our sweet August – you all are the biggest blessings of my life. Each one of you has brought a distinct light into my life, teaching me, inspiring me, and reminding me daily of the unyielding power of love and the importance of growing and learning together.

I owe a huge thank you to my parents, Michael and Portia Brown, who have always been there with open arms and hearts full of love, no matter the circumstance. Your lifetime of unconditional love, lessons, and unwavering support have shaped me into the man I am today. To my siblings, your encouragement and sibling camaraderie, through good and bad times, have been an endless source of strength.

This book is a reflection of the love, lessons, and values you all have instilled in me. It's a tribute to the unwavering belief that every setback is a setup for a comeback, a belief that has been reinforced by the constant presence and support of my beloved family, friends and mentors.

With boundless gratitude and love - Jake.

Always remember - fail forward.